COUNTRY LIVING

Perfect Patterns

FOR WALLS, FLOORS, FABRIC AND FURNITURE

COUNTRY LIVING

Perfect Patterns

FOR WALLS, FLOORS, FABRIC AND FURNITURE

Marie Proeller Hueston

HEARST BOOKS
A division of Sterling Publishing Co., Inc.

New York / London
www.sterlingpublishing.com

Design by Gretchen Scoble Design

Library of Congress Cataloging-in-Publication Data

Proeller Hueston, Marie.
Country living : perfect patterns for walls, floors, fabric & furniture /
Marie Proeller Hueston.
p. cm.
Includes index.
ISBN 978-1-58816-665-4
1. Decoration and ornament, Rustic. 2. Repetitive patterns (Decorative arts) in interior decoration. I. Country living (New York, N.Y.)
II. Title. III. Title: Perfect patterns for walls, floors, fabric & furniture.
NK1986.R8P76 2008
747--dc22
2008007842

10 9 8 7 6 5 4 3 2 1

Published by Hearst Books
A division of Sterling Publishing Co., Inc.
387 Park Avenue South, New York, NY 10016

Country Living and Hearst Books are trademarks of Hearst Communications, Inc.

www.countryliving.com

For information about custom editions, special sales, premium and corporate purchases,
please contact Sterling Special Sales Department at 800-805-5489 or specialsales@sterlingpublishing.com.

Distributed in Canada by Sterling Publishing
c/o Canadian Manda Group, 165 Dufferin Street
Toronto, Ontario, Canada M6K 3H6

Distributed in Australia by Capricorn Link (Australia) Pty. Ltd.
P.O. Box 704, Windsor, NSW 2756 Australia

Manufactured in China

Sterling ISBN 978-1-58816-665-4

Contents

Foreword

When I think of country patterns, so many beautiful images come to mind. There are colorful quilts, checked tablecloths, hooked rugs, Beacon blankets, ticking stripe, spatterware—the list goes on and on. Homes filled with pattern are warm and welcoming, but with so much to choose from, it can be difficult to decide what's right for you.

Every month in *Country Living,* we visit homes decorated with great personal flair. Some homeowners prefer period patterns and try to be as authentic as possible, down to choosing wallpapers block printed by hand and historically accurate fabrics and paint colors. Other are more eclectic in their approach, combining the prints they love most from various eras to create a style all their own. What's paramount in either case is that they are true to themselves—that's what gives the rooms you see in our magazine a sense of individuality.

Country Living Perfect Patterns is a collection of some of my favorite interiors where pattern plays a prominent role. There are spaces that overflow with flowers and teem with toile; in other rooms, a few well-placed throw pillows provide the only pattern to be found. It's my hope that all the ideas you see here offer inspiration for bringing more pattern into your home. Enjoy!

NANCY MERNIT SORIANO
Editor-in-Chief

A selection of vintage red-and-white textiles brings a sense of importance to this cozy guest room. Stripes in the form of the ticking pillow and the broader brown-and-white blanket balance the more graphic prints on the bed and echo the lines of the room's beaded board paneling.

Introduction

The patterns we choose for our homes are as influential to the overall décor as our furniture, collections, and color schemes. Patterns add vibrancy and personality to rooms. They can be used in traditional places—on a plush sofa or flowing drapes, for example—and in unexpected spots such as lampshades and cabinet knobs. Best of all, you can use as much or as little of them as you like to create one-of-a-kind interiors in which patterns make the boldest of statements, act merely as an accent, or rest comfortably in between.

An appreciation for pattern is woven into the history of the American home. In Colonial days, wealthy residences were resplendent with fine printed fabrics and graphic floor coverings imported from Europe. Simple checked homespun brightened more modest homes, where inhabitants relied on painted decoration to emulate the look of the wallpaper, carpeting, and exotic woods common in well-to-do homes. The Victorians were unabashed in their love of pattern, leaving few surfaces in the house unembellished. What's more, nineteenth-century advances in the manufacture of just about everything related to the home meant

that more families than ever before could afford to dress their homes in the prevalent style of the day.

Through the years, patterns in home furnishing have paralleled the design sensibilities of the times in which they were made: the elegant flourishes of Art Nouveau, the sleek geometrics of Art Deco, the futuristic motifs of the 1950s, the stylized florals of the 1970s, and so on. Today many of these historic and retro patterns are being reproduced while vintage bolts and swatches wait to be discovered at flea markets and antiques shops. Factor in the new patterns that regularly appear on the market and the result is an almost limitless array of options. While a boon for decorators, too many choices can also be intimidating. Where does one begin? What kind of pattern is appropriate for a particular space? How can different patterns be combined harmoniously?

Country Living Perfect Patterns can help. On the pages ahead you'll find photographs of pattern-filled interiors as well as clear instructions on how to implement the looks in your home. We've divided the vast scope of household patterns into four main categories: stripes, checks and plaids, florals, and

One of the joys of decorating with pattern is the layering effect that can be achieved when you mix and match favorite prints. One key to successfully pairing prints without overpowering a room is to limit the colors you use. Here, reds and browns are the principal hues in this living room, where checks, stripes, paisley, kilim, and other patterns peacefully coexist. Hints of blue and green are visible in the floral curtains, the carpet, and the quilt draped over one of the armchairs. A small throw pillow on the sofa echoes the sunflower-yellow accent wall, while square tiles adhered to the face of the mantel spread pattern around the room.

pictorials. Each chapter illustrates the myriad ways creative homeowners have interpreted the theme, from spreading a pattern throughout a room by adorning walls, floors, and furniture to concentrating it in a small area such as on throw pillows or a collection on display.

Which patterns will you choose to work with? Inspiration is all around, from your closet (a favorite blouse, perhaps) to your garden (a fragrant bloom) to your home library (colorful end papers). Making an inspiration board is a good way to home in on what you like best; pin snippets of fabric, wallpaper swatches, paint samples, even snapshots and postcards to a bulletin board. If you'd like to carry these items with you for reference as you visit fabric stores and flea markets, transform a thin, soft-cover photo album into an "inspiration album."

Before we begin our journey, a few general rules bear repeating. As with any decorating project, a room's scale will affect the patterns you choose. Big, bold prints tend to work best in large spaces; petite motifs thrive in cozier surroundings. Also, if you find yourself unsure where to start, it can be helpful to locate a room's focal point, whether it's the living room sofa, the master bedroom's stately four-poster, or the kitchen banquette. Choosing just the right pattern for this spot can set the tone for the entire space and guide your choices as you move outward into the room.

Finally, because fabrics supply a major source of pattern in the home, each chapter will take special care to point out the possibilities—and the pitfalls—of using them. Certain terms used by upholsterers will come in handy when shopping for and working with fabrics. One example is the ground, or background color. Correctly identifying the ground color of a busy print (is it seashell pink or mauve?) can be important when coordinating with solid-color furnishings. Likewise, finding and measuring a pattern repeat, or the complete design unit that is repeated down the length of a fabric, can help determine how much yardage will be needed for upholstery projects.

Whether you're looking for fresh ways to position the cheerful prints already in your home or you're just beginning to explore the decorating potential of pattern, *Country Living Perfect Patterns* will give you the necessary know-how to go forward with confidence.

ABOVE LEFT: Pretty wallpaper and putty-colored woodwork combine to create a serene bath. Suspended from a peg rail beside the pedestal sink, striped bags hold makeup and toiletries in style; ridged items on the ledge up above (scallop shell, creamer, footed bowl) echo the stripes of the bags.

ABOVE RIGHT: Some people are intimidated by pattern, thinking perhaps that its use implies only bold prints and busy overall schemes. But pattern in the home can be subtle as well, as this vignette illustrates. Pattern can be found in a simply painted floor pattern or in the carved or cut-out design on a wooden chair. A still life of pewter, pears, and blue-and-white china underscores the space's Early American character.

OPPOSITE: Though seen most frequently on fabric and wallpaper, household pattern can take many forms, like this collection of antique plates and platters displayed above a living room sofa. Not only does each piece deserve attention (even the all-white platters have delicately scalloped edges), but the overall arrangement on the wall also becomes a pattern in its own right.

OPPOSITE: The use of pattern in the home can be period perfect or playful, pared down or completely over the top. This sunny eating area is a good example of one homeowner's personal vision. A unique linoleum design incorporating large shapes, mismatched fabrics on the window seat, and a vase with wiggly glaze all work together to enliven the space.

ABOVE LEFT: A medley of fabrics is a favorite way to bring pattern to a room. Here, stripes, florals, polka dots, and other prints create a unified whole. The common thread? The green-and-brown color scheme. Consider the whole room, floor to ceiling, when choosing fabric for your own home. Upholstered furniture and curtains are two natural places for fabrics to enhance;

lampshades and even chandelier shades are spots that sometimes get overlooked.

ABOVE RIGHT: To the creative homeowner, walls are blank canvases; the possibilities for pattern as endless as their imaginations. There are traditional takes on painted wall patterns, such as Early American murals, and modern interpretations, like the yellow-on-lavender diamonds in this cheerful bedroom. On the bed, a vintage yo-yo quilt adds pattern as well as texture to the scene. Other touches throughout the room include the floral throw pillows, crocheted vanity-seat cover, plaid reading chair and ottoman, mismatched rugs, quilt rack, and vintage mannequin dressed with a frock.

CHAPTER ONE

Stripes

‹‹—‹

Stripes are truly an all-American pattern, from the red-and-white bands that grace Old Glory to the rows of corn and wheat that crisscross the heartland. In the home, stripes can look classic (think navy and white on an overstuffed armchair) or playful (throw pillows in sherbet-colored stripes punctuating an all-white space). No matter how they are used, stripes are a timeless country look.

· ·

A narrow red-and-white stripe fabric was chosen for the comfortable love seats in this living room. The red is repeated in the throw pillows and valances, making the fabric variations work together as a whole. This traditional take on stripes can be reinterpreted with other colors, like all blue-and-white stripes or all black-and-white. The accent fabrics for pillows and valances can even be a different pattern altogether, such as toile or chintz, and still coordinate well with the dominant stripe of the love seats. Notice how the collections in the room mirror the stripes around them, namely the brass candlesticks on the mantel and the antique slat-back chair by the window.

By nature, stripes have the ability to alter the appearance of whatever they cover, accentuating the height or width of furniture, walls, and windows, depending on whether they are placed vertically or horizontally. This is important to keep in mind when deciding where to use stripes. Long vertical bands at the windows or on the walls can make low-ceilinged rooms feel loftier. Likewise, using a wide, horizontal stripe on a cozy love seat can give the piece a grander look.

Of all the patterns shown in this book, stripes are the easiest to apply to the walls by hand using painter's tape, a level, and a ruler. The width of wall stripes is entirely up to you. Spacious rooms can handle broad bands; small dressing areas and powder rooms are particularly well suited to narrow stripes. Striped wallpaper can also create a dramatic look. If floor-to-ceiling stripes are too much for you, consider leaving the lower portion of the wall white and installing wainscoting.

The inherent linear quality of stripes makes upholstering with striped fabric a challenge. Bands need not only be perfectly aligned with the outline of any piece of furniture, they must also create a continuous line from the back of a chair or sofa, down the front of the cushion, ending at the deck, or flat platform under the cushion. If working with an upholsterer, it may be helpful to know

that draping a striped fabric vertically on furniture is called "waterfalling," while running it horizontally is called "railroading."

One of the most popular striped fabrics in country decorating is ticking. Made up of a narrow stripe set between two thinner ones, this diagonally woven cotton twill was designed to prevent feathers from poking out of mattresses and pillows. Blue-, tan-, and red-on-white are the most familiar color combinations and the most frequently found vintage examples. Owing to the pattern's popularity in recent years, manufacturers now make ticking in nearly every color, including green, yellow, and purple. Be sure to wash ticking before making any covers or curtains, as the fabric is not commonly preshrunk.

When mixing striped fabrics with other patterns, seek out a common thread to keep the look clean. A similar color combination can be effective, whether combining a variety of stripes or pairing stripes with another pattern (red-and-white stripes with a red rosebud print, for instance). Be conscious of the width of your stripes; stripes of an exaggerated width tend to look best with bold patterns like oversized flowers, while thinner stripes look ideal alongside a more traditional pattern like toile.

A bold striped carpet acts as a foundation for a bedroom dominated by red and white. The stripes' generous scale and visual strength ground the flurry of mismatched patterns up above—a combination of florals, checks, and toile. The restful brown walls and warm wood tones scattered throughout the room keep the red and white from overpowering the space. Above the mantel, a framed fabric remnant is transformed into a work of art.

ABOVE LEFT: Stripes at their simplest: A trio of throw pillows tops the bed in this neutral setting. Peg rails like the one above the bed can be invaluable resources in small rooms, holding extra clothing and decorative accessories with equal flair. In an interior where stripes are used, peg rails can also be appreciated for the strong horizontal band they add to the scene.

ABOVE RIGHT: A tower of patterned pillows is both practical and pretty in a room. This selection is arranged by size, with a range of designs unified by a red-and-white color scheme. Combined with a color-coordinated swatch of toile in a frame and a botanical print carpet, the pillows provide a lively touch in the all-white space.

OPPOSITE: Though its origins are humble, ticking stripe can be incorporated into the most elegant of settings today. Here, it is trimmed with lace and combined with toile and matelassé to dress an antique daybed. A whitewashed garden ladder becomes an attractive display for a collection of monogrammed hand towels, adding delicate patterning up above.

ABOVE: A striped settee rests in the center of a nautical-themed cottage living room. Its ocean-blue bands are a natural complement to the blue rug underfoot. In the corner, a vintage American flag stands at attention, adding another layer of stripes to the scene. Red fabric-covered lampshades and a pair of weathered shutters flanking the window ensure that no surface goes unembellished.

OPPOSITE: Hand-painted orange and yellow stripes imbue a small bedroom with personal style. The striking background sets the stage for strong accessories like a chandelier and canopy of mosquito netting. In place of a citrus-hued bedcover, which would have resulted in an overly coordinated look, is a quilted design dominated by shades of rose and olive. With so much visual drama on the walls already, artwork was kept to a minimum; a pair of framed images in the corner beside the bed provides just the right touch of additional ornament.

Using the same stripe on all furnishings in a room can result in a monotonous look. A more lively mix can be achieved by choosing a strong stripe for the sofa and a narrower design for side chairs. In this sun-drenched living room, a third stripe variation dresses throw pillows. On the floor, the woven rug underscores the room's blue-and-white color scheme; whitewashing the floorboards makes the patterns in the room stand out even more.

ABOVE LEFT. Choosing a single color scheme—in this case black and white—is a simple way to make mismatched patterns work together as a whole. Here, a thin stripe forms the base of this sofa arrangement that also includes a rooster motif as well as a graphic weave pattern behind the pillows. This look could easily be reinterpreted in blue and white, red and white, or any two-toned combination.

ABOVE RIGHT: Bed skirts are often overlooked as ideal spots to add a touch of pattern to a bedroom. (In a home office, a bed skirt on a daybed can hide file boxes and office supplies.) The narrow stripe shown here complements the blue and white bedding above. Consider the textures of the fabrics and decorative accessories you choose; wonderfully tactile grass carpeting and a matelassé bed cover possess patterns all their own.

ABOVE LEFT: Positioned below a sunny window and beside a warm fireplace, a wing chair upholstered in a red-and-white stripe creates a cozy reading nook. Pale blue paint on the chair's frame is a playful touch in an otherwise formal setting. The floral rug and toile pillow and lampshade share the upholstery fabric's cherry-red hue, inviting the eye to move around the room. Patterning even extends to the paint-decorated side table and embellished lock-box that supports the dog statuette.

ABOVE RIGHT: There are many ways stripes can play a supporting role in a room—adorning a slip-covered ottoman and the back of a wing chair are just two examples. Look closely: Even the welting, or trim, on the blue chair in the foreground has a small stripe. Hung floor to ceiling, the open shelves against the back wall assume the appearance of stripes; the interaction of white McCoy pottery and books arranged vertically and horizontally adds to the room's casual chic.

Patriotic flair permeates every inch of this airy living room. To set the stage, two different red-and-white striped fabrics were chosen for the sofa and wing chair; the rug beneath the ottoman reinforces the "broad stripes" up above. Onto this foundation, all manner of flag-inspired accessory has been placed, including throw pillows, framed flags and folk art, even a vintage bathing suit mounted on "bright stars." A blue painted ladder leans against the wall, its unadorned rungs becoming stripes of another sort.

WHY IT WORKS

❶ Broad, hand-painted pink-and-white stripes on one wall set the tone as well as the color scheme for this bedroom. The other walls were left white to keep the bold stripes from overpowering the small space.

❷ The pink-and-white stripes on the bed's head- and footboards echo the striped wall; the smaller scale balances the larger stripe while adding an element of daintiness to the setting.

❸ A braided rug beside the bed adds a hint of stripe underfoot.

❹ The floral pattern on the bed and the child's chair pairs well with the stripes in the room; the unifying element in this room is the color—shades of pink bring together the variety of patterns.

❺ A framed swatch of rose-patterned fabric breaks up the room's strong vertical lines and moves the eye around the space from bed to chair to wall.

Hand-painted stripes on walls can be wide or narrow, soft colored or bold hued. Broad cream and pale yellow bands are the perfect complement to this bedroom's flea-market furnishings, including a pair of iron beds and a collection of pillows and bedcovers.

Finishing touches lie in the accessories: checked lampshades reflect the wall's color scheme while a floral rug continues the room's springtime feeling.

◄ **TIP** *One benefit of decorating with vintage textiles is that patterns need not match exactly to look good together.*

OPPOSITE: The horizontal stripe used to cover this padded headboard mirrors stripes that occur naturally in the room, like the walls' beaded board paneling and the exposed beams overhead. A single throw pillow is carefully positioned so that its stripes run vertically for contrast.

⤙ **TIP** *Changing the slipcover on your headboard is an easy way to update the bedroom décor.*

ABOVE: Black-and-white striped wallpaper and matching draperies make a dramatic statement in this bedroom. With such a strong backdrop, furniture and accessories that are equally formidable look the most compatible. Here, dark wood furnishings, antique paintings, and a display of old photographs hold their own within the eye-catching interior. On the bed, crisp white sheets mixed with a delicate black-and-white check allow the eye a place to rest.

OPPOSITE: Because beds are the focal point of bed-rooms, they are natural spots to showcase favorite patterns. This subtle take on striped bedding incorpo-rates two red-and-white striped pillows placed beneath two blue-and-white striped pillows and a hint of a matching stripe on the bed's platform below. This arrangement can be reinterpreted in endless ways to match a room's overall decor; some people might choose more vivid colors for either the solids or the stripes while others might replace the solid bedding with a floral or checked print.

ABOVE: In a pale blue kitchen, patterned fabrics add a punch of color. The wide stripe on the right side of the banquette echoes the red of the matching pair of pillows; the blue-and-yellow stripe keeps the arrange-ment from being overly symmetrical. A blue-and-white striped Cornishware pitcher holds fresh flowers on the table. Weathered wood surfaces, like the ones on the stool and the cupboard, possess a pattern all their own.

ABOVE AND OPPOSITE: Though we may be most familiar with stripes that feature white and a single color, a broad spectrum of striped patterns is available to homeowners today. In this open living/dining area, a color-rich stripe reflects the sea, sky, and vegetation visible just outside the picture windows. On the sofa, an energetic effect is achieved by alternating horizontal and vertical placement of pillows. In the far corner of the room, a single slip-covered side chair is positioned beneath a large framed print to create an artful vignette. Slipcovered chairs also surround a round table in the dining area; remnants of the fabric were fashioned into place mats for a coordinated table setting.

Slipcovers fashioned from black-and-white ticking stripe dress a camelback sofa. The simplicity of the pattern is an ideal match for the understated elegance of the room. Pillows in both a matching stripe and a wider design add depth to the arrangement. Ticking-stripe pillows are also positioned on the white armchair, moving the pattern around the room.

How to Create a Striking Mix

❶ To give different patterns a common thread, limit color choices to one or two hues. Here, deep plum stripes and toile are paired with several shades of red.

❷ Spread dominant patterns around the room—don't group them close together. The stripe on the two armchairs also adorns the sofa cushion; the toile drapes find a partner in the seat of the wood-framed armchair; the soft red check that covers the ottoman was also used on the long sofa cushion.

❸ Confine especially bold or striking patterns to small furniture or accessories, then place them prominently in the room. A white-on-red throw pillow draws attention to the center of the sofa.

OPPOSITE: Slipper chairs covered in a red-and-white stripe stand at the head and foot of a dining table, bringing the elegance of a formal dining room to this sun-drenched corner of an open great room. A complementary color scheme unifies the stripe and the lattice pattern used on the other seat cushions.

ABOVE: A number of factors can affect the choice of stripe for a particular space—sometimes the character of the room itself makes one type of stripe seem like the right option, other times personal preference takes highest priority. In this Scandinavian-inspired living room, it was the antique sofa frame that inspired the upholstery fabric; the timeworn wood surface suggested a palette of faded hues and fabrics with a slightly rumpled appearance. The body of the sofa was covered in a tan-and-brown stripe, while a pictorial pattern was used for the seat cushion. A trio of pillows rests up top—two in a darker stripe, one in an embroidered floral motif. Using multiple patterns on a single piece of furniture evokes an heirloom that's been passed down in the family for generations.

DECORATING WITH OLD GLORY

Arguably the most recognizable symbol in America, our nation's flag is also a popular motif in interior design. Small wonder, considering the flag's unique combination of bold colors and strong graphics. Decorating with Old Glory is simple and can be done in a manner that is low key—a single framed flag hung on the wall, perhaps—or delightfully over the top. If taking the latter route, start with a broad red-and-white stripe on a sofa, armchair, or duvet. From this central point, you can move outward, adding whatever you'd like: star-trimmed curtains,

needlepoint throw pillows, even a cluster of parade flags arranged in an old jelly jar.

Look for vintage flags and flag memorabilia at flea markets, antiques shops, and thrift stores. Flag-inspired folk art, made by creative folks throughout our nation's history, can be a whimsical touch as well. Finally, because so many home accessories are available in red and white or blue and white, feel free to incorporate these color-coordinated, though not necessarily flag-themed, items as they will be natural partners with the overall scheme.

To capture the spirit of our nation's flag in any room in the house, one need only combine red-and-white striped fabrics with blue-and-white designs, especially any prints that feature stars. Attaching curtain rings to a red, white, and blue banner or a length of flag-themed fabric makes a simple curtain. Keep an eye out for patriotic folk art like the small star, button flag, and Lady Liberty on the wall beside the window.

Whimsy and formality meet in this living room awash in green, lavender, and yellow. A broad green stripe was chosen for the sofas; their seat cushions are covered in the thin purple stripe of the armchair nearby.

Narrow purple stripes can be seen on the sofas' welting and in the thin stripe going down the center of the woven rug. On the mantel, the horizon lines on a trio of sunset landscapes act as another set of stripes.

The fine art of combining different patterns can be carried out by piling a sofa with pillows. Acting as a foundation for all the other prints is a quilted couch cover in stripes of red, beige, and brown. Onto this, other patterns are placed, all bearing a similar red-and-brown color scheme. The ottoman just in front of the couch is covered with the same checked fabric of the outermost pillows. The tassel-edged pillow repeats the fruit and flower fabric of the drapes. In the center of the arrangement are kilim covers, a solid light-brown pillow trimmed with red, and a single yellow square that reflects the color of the wall.

ABOVE: Patterns can become the main attraction in a room or they can act merely as an accent. In this all-white dining room, a hint of color is found in the stripes of the woven rug. The eye also reads the wide planks of the dining table and architectural elements like the exposed beams as additional stripes.

OPPOSITE: Mismatched stripes in this sunroom are held together by the deep-red hue each of them shares; the mixture of broad and thin bands on fabrics and rug energizes the scene. A touch of floral pattern is introduced in the center of the red-and-white striped pillows on the settee.

Collections can be a creative way to incorporate favorite patterns into a setting. In this whitewashed kitchen, long open shelves harbor a neatly arranged collection of 1920s Cornishware. In addition to large displays like this one, a single item or small grouping of collectibles on a mantel, sink top, or side table can mirror a room's dominant pattern.

HANGING PLATES ON THE WALL

Sometimes it is only when we take something out of its traditional setting that we can truly appreciate its aesthetic qualities. Such is the case when saucers, plates, and platters are lifted off the dinner table and displayed on the wall. Beyond their original function, many plates are also small works of art with imagery as diverse as fruit, flowers, people, polka dots, birds, bumblebees, stars, landscapes, and national monuments—all perfect for adding a punch of pattern to a space.

Wall-mounted plates look great over a sideboard or dining table as well as in unexpected places (above a bed or running the length of a hallway, perhaps). The hardware you'll need can usually be found at art supply and hardware stores. Before you hammer a single nail, it's a good idea to create paper templates of each plate and play with placement either on the floor or on the wall, using nonstaining art putty. Move the templates around until you find an arrangement that works best for you. Grids, casual clusters, and simple rows, either horizontal or vertical, are all common compositions. The amount of space you have to work with and your own personal taste will guide your placement decisions.

CHAPTER TWO

Checks and Plaids

⊷

Ever since the sound of looms click-clacked through the lanes of Colonial villages, checked fabrics have been a mainstay in American homes. Back then, blue-and white and brown-and-white checked homespun hung at windows and covered bed "ticks" filled with feathers. Today, checked fabrics continue to grace windows, beds, and many other spots in our homes, proving the timelessness of what might be called the quintessential country pattern.

Decorative paint and a simple checked fabric make a powerful statement in this rustic interior. Because the arrangement is so pared down, the choice of bold colors—deep red and crisp blue and white—was vital to make the visual impact as strong as possible. A small striped pillow provides the perfect finishing touch.

While simple in design, the range of checked and plaid fabrics on the market today is broad, encompassing old-fashioned home-spun and petite gingham to pastel madras and jewel-toned tartan. Just as endless as the varieties to be found are the ways checks and plaids can be used around the house: a red-and-white tablecloth on a kitchen table, gingham curtains in a child's room, a nine-patch quilt on a bed, a checked lamp-shade, a cozy plaid wool blanket draped over the back of a sofa or wing chair. A number of our familiar visions of checks and plaids in the home were not made of fabric at all, including painted checkerboard floor patterns and the check- and plaid-motif kitchen canisters, cookie tins, and other accessories made over the years.

A refreshing green-and-white check dresses a love seat and ottoman, creating a welcoming alcove ideal for reading, sewing, or simply relaxing. A self-welt applied on the diagonal, or in candy cane style, adds visual interest. A pretty quilt rests on top of the ottoman, ready for use on chilly days. The quilt's floral pattern echoes the floral motif of the wallpaper; the pink blossoms add an extra blush of color to the scene.

Vintage quilts were recycled into one-of-a-kind covers for this bedroom's slipper chair and footstool. The quilt pattern was positioned so its checks created a border around the back and seat of the chair; a portion of the textile that includes larger squares was used for the gathered skirt. The simplicity and crisp red-and-white color scheme of the furniture pairs well with the oversize painting of a white farmhouse with red picket fence.

Checked fabric is an important element in the popular Swedish country look. Known for a pared-down aesthetic and pale woodwork and walls, Swedish country interiors often featured a two-tone color scheme, frequently red and white or blue and white. To re-create the look in your own home, try positioning a wood-frame settee upholstered in checked fabric in the living room or covering the seats of dining-room or kitchen chairs with a similar kind of check (especially if the chair frames are painted white or putty color). Dress windows with sheer white curtains or hang a simple lace valance to finish the look.

As with stripes, upholstering with checks and plaid fabrics requires a bit of skill to ensure that the straight edges of the pattern are aligned with the furniture frame and that the lines extend straight down the chair or sofa backs to the front of the cushion. Plaids can be especially tricky, as slight irregularities are so often part of their charm. This is especially true of madras, a cotton plaid that originated in India. Madras commonly displays weaving discrepancies that make it ill-suited to very structured pieces of furniture where lines must meet exactly. Rather, fans of madras should save the bright-hued fabric for tablecloths, throw pillows, curtains, and big comfy chairs used primarily for curling up with a good book.

OPPOSITE, TOP: In bedrooms where space is an issue—like this cozy nest tucked beneath the eaves—concentrate pattern on the bed by choosing beautiful sheets, quilts, and pillow shams. Though the six-point star pattern of this quilt commands the most attention, the checked throw pillow and matching lampshade hold their own. The patchwork pillow sham and bedsheet form a secondary checked pattern, while a trio of black-and-white photographs brings a similar sensibility to the walls. The red-and-white floral bedding that peeks out here and there softens the edges of the overall arrangement.

OPPOSITE, BOTTOM: A classic indigo-and-white check is the ideal accompaniment to a bedroom decorated in traditional Early American style. The inside of the scalloped canopy was left white to create a serene view from underneath; the bed curtains are pulled to the back, creating a headboard of sorts. The crisscross of the blue-and-white throw pillow draws the eye down; a pile of checked homespun rests on a wallpaper-covered box on the nightstand. Other period patterns sharing the space include the coverlet and ticking stripe pillow on the love seat, the carpet, and the delicate stencil along the top of the walls.

The simple beauty of checked fabric makes it the ideal accompaniment to just about any other pattern. Mixtures look best when the different fabrics share a main color scheme or when the check picks up a secondary color in another fabric (imagine green-and-white gingham paired with a rose pattern with pale green leaves. Scale is another important factor in the successful combination of fabrics; in general, the scale of a check should be approximately the same as that of the other motifs in an arrangement. The deeper hues of tartan plaids along with their wintry feel makes them best suited to mixing and matching with darker colors and richly textured fabrics. Using a number of plaids together in the same scheme is another attractive option.

OPPOSITE: A bit more intricate than a simple black-and-white checkerboard floor pattern, this variation features faux marbling in both the black and white squares. The floor was intentionally left unvarnished so that it would acquire an antiqued appearance over time.

◄◄ **TIP** *To achieve a timeworn finish on painted floors, leave them unvarnished and exposed to the everyday foot traffic in your home.*

ABOVE: A living room decorated in traditional Swedish country style features a wood-frame settee uphol-stered in a simple blue-and-white check. In the fore-ground, the backs of two armchairs reveal a color-coordinated striped pattern. The pale blue tone applied beneath the darker wainscoting adds an extra dash of color to the room; typical of Swedish style, arrangements on walls and tabletops are kept spare throughout the space.

OPPOSITE: Patterns do not have to be used in large quantities to make a strong impact on a room. In this bedroom, a bold blue plaid on a headboard and armchair was enough to create an eye-catching interior. The fabric's hue set against the light mustard of the walls offers a fresh twist on the popular color combination of blue and yellow. A Gothic-style wooden side chair dressed in a delicate pattern of its own doubles as a nightstand.

ABOVE: So timeless is a simple blue-and-white checked fabric that its use as a curtain in this bath is a perfect accompaniment to other formal details such as the chandelier, wall sconce, and silver vase. A color-coordinated toile curtain with a white liner completes the window dressing.

ABOVE: Scale is an important factor when determining the best pattern for an interior. To stand out in this dining area filled with strong silhouettes and dark woods, the check on the chairs needed to be sizable. The clean lines of the pattern mirror the room's pared-down aesthetic; the color scheme echoes the kitchen's blue woodwork. At the windows, an elegant pictorial fabric (also of a larger scale) picks up the blue used throughout the room and adds a touch of sunny yellow.

OPPOSITE: A checkerboard floor pattern in an unexpected purple-and-white palette is a fresh twist on a classic country detail. A darker shade of purple is used above the walls' beaded board paneling. Behind the tub, a checkerboard of colorful tiles that brings in all hues used in the room is a lovely finishing touch. Don't overlook the pattern potential of towels and bathmats, like the green-and-white stripe used here.

Why It Works

❶ At the window, new curtains call to mind historic homespun, a natural choice for a traditional country setting such as this.

❷ A blue-and-white checked duvet reflects the hues of the room's antique furniture and accessories, including the folk art doll, the blue-painted drawers above it, and the calico-covered book on the nightstand.

❸ Two piles of pillows add a contemporary sensibility to the scene.

❹ The quilt's large squares underscore the room's pattern theme; folding the top down ensures that the smaller checks in the room are the main focus of attention.

Plaid aficionados are certain to appreciate this whimsical cottage living room, where a variety of tartans and floral fabrics have been combined. Red tartan covers the top of the walls above the white beaded board. Roman shades of red-and-green plaid on a beige ground stand out against the walls. Notice the red rickrack used to tie up the shades. Another plaid with thinner bands of beige covers a footstool (visible just below the yellow table). Throw pillows include a red-and-black plaid on the green wing chair at the right and a green, red, and white on the sofa. Collections complete the look; vintage metal picnic baskets and thermoses sit on top of the corner cabinet and the yellow table. Stripes of green and red embellish the whitewashed armoire, while hunter green velvet welting gives a wintry feeling to the sofa's red floral fabric.

ABOVE LEFT: A wallpaper pattern of world flags takes on the appearance of a small-scale tile pattern. The adjoining room's schooner wallpaper is visible in the mirror. To balance the busy pattern on the walls, other details were kept simple: white sink, vintage medicine cabinet, and monogrammed hand towels.

⤙ **TIP** *Small spaces like bathrooms, dressing rooms, and hallways are good choices for busy or exuberant wallpaper because the patterns are experienced for limited periods of time. In a space that's used frequently, a vibrant pattern could become irritating, but used in a space that's visited briefly, it can be delightful.*

ABOVE RIGHT: Plaid sheets in soft greens and blues set a masculine tone in this cozy bedroom. White bedspreads and an additional blue pillow give the arrangement easy elegance, as if pieced together from the linen closet. Even the matching bed frames are adorned with pattern.

A red-and-tan plaid fabric on the sofa and a color-coordinated check on the armchair beside it evoke classic country style. The off-white throw pillows on the sofa hem in the wide horizontal bands of the plaid. The graphic roman shade adds a curvaceous quality to the scene.

FOLDING SCREENS

One of the most versatile accessories for the home, folding screens provide an element of privacy in any room. In bedrooms they can delineate a dressing area, in living rooms they can hide a television, in dining rooms they can shelter a sideboard filled with food, in family rooms they can designate one corner as a home office. In addition to their inherent practicality, folding screens are also ideal for infusing an interior with pattern—their vertical panels can be coordinated to match any décor.

New folding screens can be found in home design stores, while vintage examples occasionally surface at flea markets and antiques stores. Handy folks can even make their own using hinged panels of furniture-grade plywood (a height of 12 to 18 inches below the ceiling is common) decorated with fabric, wallpaper, or a painted pattern on the side that will face the room. You can even put a pattern on both sides (a floral on one side, a coordinating stripe on the other) to change the screen's look on a whim. When buying vintage screens, a certain degree of wear and fading is to be expected. Some people prefer this timeworn look; in such cases, simply wipe the screen down with a damp cloth before positioning it in its new home.

If you have a favorite color scheme, by all means run with it when choosing patterns for your home. In this sunny living room, nearly a dozen different prints on fabrics, floor, and collections all share a classic blue-and-white combination. Traditional patterns—the plaid drapes, the checked floor pattern, the checkerboard throw pillows, and the pieced quilt—balance the more contemporary designs on the sofas and armchair.

ABOVE: Blue-and-white check lines the inside of a pair of wing chairs that have a bird and flower motif on the outside. The unexpected combination of patterns provides a modern twist on the traditional American country interior. The woven rug beneath the table continues the check motif as well as the blue-and-white color scheme. Graniteware buckets used as vases on the table and standing in the fireplace, and star motif vases above the mantel add punches of pattern throughout the space.

OPPOSITE: In this sunny bath, black-and-white floor tiles and a loose, hand-painted grid on the walls present a playful take on checked patterns. A similar wall design would be easy to re-create with a wide brush and any paint color you wish. Striped shades give the windows a tailored appearance. The walls' sunflower hue is repeated in the painted "bath rug" and slip-covered chair and on the painted woodwork, interior shutters, and tub base, giving the busy décor a cohesive look.

OPPOSITE: When a room's patterns are particularly busy or when multiple collections vie for attention, a simple checked floor pattern can be a grounding element. Such is the case in this dining room where enamelware occupies the top of a sideboard and the space below it. The blue of the woven checked rug is repeated in the enamelware collection, the tableware, and the folding screen.

ABOVE: A small desk and a slipper chair are all that are needed to transform any sunny window into a pretty spot for letter writing, crafts, or quiet contemplation. The trio of patterns seen here—a large-scale gingham on the chair, a petite motif on the windows, and an open floral on the throw—work well together and can be reinterpreted in other color schemes (blue chair and drapes with a yellow throw, for example, or green chair and drapes with a lavender throw).

A neutral plaid rug serves as the foundation for a living room awash in beige, warm browns, and hints of red. Similar woven patterns underfoot can coordinate with any color scheme in a room. Rugs like this can even be used to unify different colored furnishings as long as each hue is woven into the rug.

How to Create a Striking Mix

❶ Choose a dominant color, such as the deep red that touches checks, stripes, and florals in this dining room.

❷ Use symmetry to establish order within a lively mix of patterns. The drapes on the right and left side of the photograph, for example, mirror one another.

❸ Move accent fabrics around the room. The plaid that's used on the left and right cornices, or upholstered valances, also forms the edge treatment on the dark-red drapes in the background.

❹ Place an eye-catching pattern in an unexpected spot, like the large check on the backs of the chairs.

❺ Keep carpeting a light color to let the strong hues in the room take center stage.

OPPOSITE: A black-and-white tile checkerboard pattern evokes a bit of café chic in this country kitchen. Covering just a small amount of space with the tiles keeps the graphic pattern from overwhelming the room; white walls and exposed beams also help balance the checks. A set of chairs with ornate carved tops and color-coordinated striped fabric surrounds the dining table.

◄← **TIP** *Enhance a kitchen backsplash, bathroom wall, or fireplace surround with a simple checkerboard of white and solid-colored tiles.*

ABOVE: Pretty as well as practical, red-and-white fabric curtains embellish cabinets and a small cupboard in this rustic kitchen. The red of the fabric is picked up in the interior of the tall shelves on the left. Other cabinet fronts on the work island have been customized with panels of pierced tin and wire mesh. The pale blue checked tablecloth on the table is a classic accessory for a country kitchen.

OPPOSITE: A small yellow-and-white check covers the sofas in this open living/dining area where a tile floor creates a checked pattern underfoot. The choice of color for the sofa fabric brings a sunny note into the space while directing attention to the view out the windows and the deep green of the window frames and dining chairs. A broad yellow stripe at the windows and accent fabrics on the throw pillows and footstool complement the sofas.

ABOVE: Choosing two neutral colors to decorate a whole room results in a serene setting, like this living room where matching futon frames bear cushions with identical covers. Checks are well-suited to such pared-down schemes: a larger beige-and-white gingham graces the front of the futon cushions, while a smaller design trims the outside. A collection of needlework pillows adds texture and color to the room.

ABOVE LEFT: Accent pillows are a simple way to add pattern to a room, whether the pattern you favor is stripes, pictorials, or checks—like the petite designs seen here. Window seats are the perfect place to line up a row of pillows; their patterns and colors can be enjoyed by those inside the house as well as by passersby.

ABOVE RIGHT: A soft take on checks can be seen in this bedroom, where a large checkerboard pattern blanket and an antique brown-and-white quilt top a whitewashed iron bed. On the wall, a loose grid pattern of vintage photographs echoes the loose checks of the bed. The sepia tones of the photographs inspired the room's color scheme.

SINK SKIRTS

Who among us couldn't use a bit of additional space to stow beauty and cleaning supplies, towels, or the countless storage boxes we fill with clothing, paperwork, photographs, and the like? Not only is a sink skirt a simple way to increase a room's storage capacity, it also adds a splash of pattern to an interior. Equally at home in a kitchen, mudroom, master bath, or powder room, sink skirts can also be used to mask table legs, expanding the possibility for stylish storage in home offices, dressing areas, and nearly every room in the house.

To begin, find a fabric you love. You'll need enough to reach around the whole sink or table, allowing for folds along the way that will create a gathered skirt feel. (For a sleeker look, you can also pull the fabric taut.) Jot down the dimensions of the sink or table, both the length around the top and the height from where the skirt will be attached to where it will reach the floor, taking into account hems you'll want to sew on the top and bottom edges. Using Super Glue, attach a length of Velcro® (available at fabric or craft stores) to the inside or outside front of the sink or table; sew the other side onto the corresponding side (front or back) of your skirt. In this way, you'll be able to remove the skirt for cleaning.

A plaid of soft red and white covers a daybed, bringing the spirit of Swedish country style to this guest room. A trio of pillows tops the bed in matching plaid, off-white, and pale green floral.

Antique game boards parade along a mantel, illustrating how collections can complement the patterns we use in our homes. The arrangement is made lively by layering small in front of large designs. Mantels are natural spots for displays like this, as they are generally the focal point of a room.

CHAPTER THREE

Florals

Perhaps it's our love affair with gardening that makes floral patterns so universally appealing. The range of prints to be found can be compared to a garden, representing every type of flower from tiny buds to full-blown blooms and every color under the sun. Floral patterns complement cozy cottages and grand manors, rural and urban settings, small powder rooms and spacious master suites. In short, they are all that's best about country decorating.

A fresh, fun take on florals can be seen in this bedroom vignette where mismatched throw pillows reflect the bright colors of the duvet. Carrying a swatch of a room's dominant fabric is a good idea when shopping for pillows; you'll be able to check if a certain stripe, solid, or floral print goes well or simply won't do. A large flower painting on the wall balances the strong colors and graphics of the bed.

There are many ways to approach decorating with floral patterns. One is flirty and feminine, with blooms covering walls, furniture, curtains, and bedding. At the opposite end of the spectrum is a more subtle take that appeals even to those who wouldn't ordinarily consider florals. Dark woods, a pared-down floor plan, and deeper shades of green, brown, or blue in place of brighter hues like red and pink characterize this simpler style. In between these two lie countless ways to make floral patterns your own.

In addition to traditional means (fabric, wallpaper, carpeting) of bringing floral patterns into the home, collections are another option to consider. Owing to their enduring popularity, floral patterns have been applied to china, ceramics, glass, silver, textiles, and many other objects over the years. Mantels, bookshelves, windowsills, and tabletops are natural places to arrange a selection of flower-themed possessions. An arch of plates on a wall, a row of teapots on a shelf, and a stack of quilts in a country cupboard are all looks you might try. The more items in a grouping, the greater the visual impact.

When upholstering with floral fabrics, the need for exact alignment is not as great as it is with linear stripes and checks. The curvaceous nature of these patterns and the inherent qualities of real flowers, stems, and vines allow for slight differences in positioning, which will not be immediately discernable and may even help the finished piece look as if the pattern were growing and meandering over its form. To coordinate a floral print with other patterned or solid-colored elements in a room, first identify the fabric's ground, or background color, especially if it is a very busy pattern. The ground color can also affect the look of a piece of furniture; darker grounds tend to give pieces more weight while pale hues result in a lighter feel. Have fun with floral fabrics: play with placement to position particular blooms in the center of a chair back or on the front of an accent pillow.

How floral prints will be mixed with other patterns in each room is a matter of personal taste. In more formal settings, a floral print might be paired with one other pattern such as a green-and-white stripe or red-and-white toile. In casual interiors, florals can share space with a number of other patterns in a more random manner. Generally, a common thread of color scheme or scale is called upon to unify florals with other patterns. Combining a variety of floral prints can also be attractive, resulting in an energetic mix that resembles a garden in bloom.

Ornate Victorian furniture is ideal for people who love floral patterns. Here, a pair of twin beds with carved flower baskets and trailing vines support nearly identical piles of accent pillows. Both new and vintage floral fabrics were used for the pillow covers. The common thread among all the fabrics is the presence of pink, a hue that is repeated on the nightstand's tissue box, lamp base, and lampshade. The celadon walls let the pink details really pop.

OPPOSITE: If you have only a small amount of a fabric you love, find a prominent spot to use it, like the vertical quartet of floral arrangements that graces this bedroom window. The patterned wallpaper and pale-blue walls are a twist on the traditional patterned walls and solid ceilings. Although no floral prints dress the bed, the rosy hues evoke a garden feel. The striped rug in the foreground picks up the faded blues and greens found elsewhere in the room.

ABOVE: Floral fabrics in the living room blur the line between indoors and out. In this sunny space, a striped rose pattern was chosen for the sofa; the same fabric was used as welting for the beige seat cushion. The rose pattern was also used as an accent around the room—as a seat cushion for the weathered cruise ship deck chair and around the sides of the armchair's cushions. Garden antiques like the wicker chair and vintage plant stand in the background are natural choices for floral interiors.

ABOVE: Floral patterns and an ornate iron bed bring an air of elegance to a bedroom under the eaves. The wall behind the bed was papered with an earth-toned floral, while the duvet's deep scarlet has a regal feel. The bed skirt's smaller print picks up the colors above. The warm ocher wall complements the room's red tones. The perfect finishing touch: a vintage leaf-and-flower chandelier positioned over the bed.

OPPOSITE: Dramatic pattern looks wonderful in dramatic spaces, like the deep-pink trellis wallpaper in this vaulted bedroom. The pure-white rafters, bedcovers, and furnishings balance the strong colors of the walls. Matching Double Wedding Ring quilts at the bottoms of the beds echo the wallpaper pattern. To focus full attention on the vibrancy above, the pine floors were left bare.

A faded rose pattern reminiscent of English country cottages was chosen for the armchairs and ottoman in this living room. Bands of solid, putty-colored fabric and dark red welting update the old-fashioned feeling of the rose print. Mismatched floral throw pillows top the beige sofa. At the windows, floral fabric with a similar ground color but with flowers of a deeper hue is casually draped to create coordinating valances. Tiffany-style lamps like the example on the wicker side table are right at home in floral settings.

The soft blue-and-white floral fabric on this living room love seat blends seamlessly into its neutral surroundings, illustrating a subtle approach to decorating with florals that would appeal even to those people who always viewed the family of patterns as overly feminine. White armchairs and a blue-and-white striped ottoman complete the ensemble of furniture set against a backdrop of dark woods and white walls.

OPPOSITE: A favorite painting and a beloved pillow personalize this charming bedroom vignette. To dress a bed in similar fashion, choose a small floral print for the fitted sheet, then top it with a pale blue sheet and a striped duvet. Stack two pillows with pale blue cases at the head of the bed and lean a striped pillow at the front. Add a throw pillow with a distinctive floral print as a finishing touch.

ABOVE: Floral prints are a popular choice for little girls' rooms. And because a mixture of different florals looks good together, the patterns are especially well suited to a room shared by two sisters with very different tastes—like the bedroom seen here. Roses bloom on one sister's side of the room; the duvet, lampshade, and vanity stool trimmed with red polka-dots are all fashioned from the same fabric. An oversize pillow covered in a pink-and-white rose print and a vintage design depicting a ring of flowers surrounding a kitten and bunny also top the bed. Nearby, the blue-and-white bed frame and patchwork quilt with darker hued florals denotes the older sister's side of the room. The red-and-white gingham bed skirt echoes the red bed frame and red polka-dot trim, creating a sense of unanimity in the space.

Papering a single wall with a rose pattern adds a touch of femininity to this bedroom without overpowering the space. Green woodwork around the windows brings out the color of the leaves. The old-fashioned style of the wallpaper complements the room's simple country style. On the bed, a small-print floral duvet continues the floral theme. A checked rug beneath the bench carries out the color scheme underfoot.

ABOVE LEFT: This attractive wall display is easy to re-create. Begin with an oval mirror (the weathered surface of this example complements the old-fashioned bedding below). Choose a pair of favorite images in pretty frames to flank the mirror. Position the bottom of the two frames slightly lower than the mirror. Next, arrange an arch of floral plates in a symmetrical manner. As a finishing touch, suspend a smaller framed image in front of the mirror with a ribbon; notice how the bottom of the smaller frame lines up with the two matching frames.

ABOVE RIGHT: Unapologetic in its femininity, this room illustrates the range of surfaces and items that can be relied upon to bring pattern into your home. Roses bloom on the walls (both on the wallpaper and the border), sofa, footstool, tea set, hatbox, circular frame, and dress. A collection of vintage floral hats underscores the garden theme. Curvaceous furniture and accessories like the side table and the green painted coat rack work well with flirty florals like these.

ABOVE LEFT: A lily-of-the-valley print covers the walls in this pretty bedroom. Furnishings and details were kept simple to focus full attention on the walls. Crisp white was chosen for bedding and curtains; light green checked fabric covers the matching headboards. A large mirror and scalloped shelf were painted a light robin's-egg blue. Wicker (like the whitewashed nightstand) and other furniture styles traditionally associated with porches and patios are especially well suited to interiors awash in floral patterns.

ABOVE RIGHT: Bedding in a bold palette of red, orange, pink, and yellow stands out against the backdrop of a soft-hued wallpaper and a poppy-red carpet. White furniture and details such as sheets and lampshades allow places for the eye to rest.

OPPOSITE: Choosing a two-tone color scheme is a simple way to unify different patterns. Blue and white in particular is a classic combination and one, with respect to an interior decorated with florals, that keeps the overall look from being too feminine. Here, florals, stripes, and checks peacefully coexist on a rustic bed. Framed floral prints and a hand-painted lamp base continue the floral theme.

OPPOSITE: Red and green is a timeless color combination; pairing deep scarlet with pale apple green is especially pleasing. In this sunny breakfast area, a rose pattern with gray-green leaves covers the cushions and pillows of a banquette. The red seat cushions and red-and-white check tablecloth draw out the red shadowing on the rose print. A selection of floral-motif plates creates an eye-catching wall display. Though each plate has a different pattern, the predominance of red and green details unifies the group as a whole and makes an ideal accompaniment to the room's color scheme.

ABOVE LEFT: Twin beds offer the opportunity to create wonderfully symmetrical decorating schemes that are easy to duplicate. Begin with matching bed frames, then dress them in coordinating bedding; here, floral pillow shams are paired with white sheets and floral-and-print patchwork quilts. Next, choose two similar paintings, prints, or photographs to hang over the beds. A nightstand or dresser positioned between the beds is the perfect finishing touch and the ideal spot for an arrangement of fresh flowers. Floral aficionados should never pass up charming and useful furnishings embellished with hand-painted blooms (like this vintage luggage rack) when they spot them at a flea market or antiques shop.

ABOVE RIGHT: Red florals, stripes, and checks set against a backdrop of deep teal make a bold statement in this bedroom. To re-create the look (with either the same color scheme or a different one), visit your local paint store armed with a swatch of a pattern that will be featured prominently in your home, then find a shade of paint for the walls that is in strong contrast with that pattern. A row of framed botanical prints is an attractive choice for any room populated by floral patterns.

The purple-and-yellow color scheme of this violet-print wallpaper is echoed around the room in solid swatches of paint and fabric. The vaulted ceiling is coated in lavender paint, while the headboard is upholstered with lavender fabric. Butter-yellow fabric was used for the seat cushions on the settee and the side chair. Bare floors and whitewashed woodwork and furnishings throughout balance the wallpaper's busy pattern.

WHY IT WORKS

❶ Shades of red in each fabric reflect the warm tone of the exposed brick wall; the floral motifs soften the wall's hard edges.

❷ Each throw pillow features a different floral pattern, giving the grouping the spirit of a collection gathered over time.

❸ Upholstered in the same fabric, a modern chair and a footstool with more traditional carved legs work as a set.

❹ Large flower paintings are natural partners with the room's overall theme.

An energetic mix of floral fabrics populates this sunroom, bringing the spirit of an overflowing flower garden indoors. Collections reinforce the room's floral theme: a row of vintage florist baskets parades along the windowsill behind the sofa, while amateur still lifes of pansies are clustered close to the ceiling. Wicker furniture is a natural choice for casual interiors decorated with floral patterns.

Don't limit your use of floral fabrics to merely upholstery and pillow covers. In this inviting living room, vintage bark cloth revives the appearance of an old blanket chest just inside the doorway; a more contemporary pattern in lavender, purple, and white covers a small box on the whitewashed side table in the foreground.

ABOVE: Having a particular theme to search for makes shopping a flea market more fun; one homeowner keeps an eye out for anything floral to use in her sunny living room. At the window, amateur still lifes line the windowsill beneath valances fashioned from a set of printed cotton napkins. Mismatched floral pillows dress the sofa and armchair. Underfoot, a floral hooked rug gives tired feet an attractive place to rest.

OPPOSITE: The use of florals in a room can be as bold or as subtle as you wish. In this spacious bedroom, its use is limited to a hooked rug on the floor and two floral-print bedspreads—one covering the bottom of a dramatic bed and the other folded beneath a white blanket on a wicker blanket chest. A row of bud vases, each holding a single stem, makes a pretty display along a mantel.

ABOVE LEFT: In this delightfully demure living room, rosebuds punctuate the wallpaper around an archway as well as the far wall of the adjoining room. Fabric with the same print was used for the archway's curtain. A larger rose print upholsters the sofa, visible in the far left foreground of the photograph. Soft green paint was applied to the wall above the archway and on the ceiling in the other room. Paint in deeper shades of rose and leaf green was also used on various furnishings in both rooms, including the lamp and small table, the armoire, and the molding. Vintage quilts were recycled to cover wing chairs. The quilt pattern on the chair beside the writing desk is aptly named: Grandmother's Flower Garden.

ABOVE RIGHT: Floral painted patterns would generally be too busy for the floor, unless they are pared down considerably like the stencil design shown here. On a ground of dark brown, blue flowers punctuate the squares created by intersecting bands of cream and red. The red is echoed in the toile seat cover up above.

Mantels are natural focal points in rooms; use them to display collections that underscore the patterns used throughout the space. Here, nineteenth-century china in pink hues and floral motifs complements the rose-and-daisy fabric on the chair in the foreground and the antique hooked rugs underfoot. A pink-and-white color scheme also unifies the living room's additional fabrics: toile on the armchair and footstool, a narrow stripe on the chaise.

SLIPCOVERS

The term "slipcover" may conjure images of an over-stuffed sofa in a room frequented by pets and small children. While slipcovers will always offer busy households a way to keep sofas clean, there is so much more that can be done with them. In the dining room, for instance, slipcovers can be put on chairs before a party begins to give the furniture a more festive feeling. (They might also be taken off the seats just prior to a party, in the interim having been protecting antique chairs from everyday use.) Pillow shams, small circular accent tables, and vanity-table

stools are just a sampling of the additional pieces of furniture that can be fitted for slipcovers. Lightweight cottons, linens, or wools are best for slipcovers—fabrics that are sturdy and easy to clean. To prevent shrinking, prewash the fabric twice in hot water, followed by two times in the dryer before the covers are sewn. Remember that slipcovers can alter the look of a room as the seasons change; covers on sofas and chairs might be white in the summer, a richly toned floral in the winter.

Crewelwork—an embroidered floral motif popular in Early America—is common in period restorations as well as contemporary interpretations of country style. Blue flowers on the crewel drapes complement the soft pumpkin hue of the sofa. Between the windows, pressed flowers in ornate antique frames pair well with the richness of the drapery fabric and the curvaceous silhouettes of the sofa and coffee table.

OPPOSITE: Since porches are extensions of the garden, what better place to use floral patterns? Mismatched floral fabrics cover the pillows piled atop a gracious daybed. Additional accent pillows in shades of red pick up the red in the floral motifs. A simple striped mattress reflects the white bands of the house's clapboard siding and the blue bands of the floorboards. A hand-painted rose graces the storage box to the right of the daybed.

ABOVE: Few things are as inviting as a bed piled high with pillows. Pale colors and plenty of off-white backgrounds keep the lively mix of fabrics from overpowering this serene space. Matching side tables with delicate hand-painted designs frame the bed's elegant headboard; the blue color of the furnishings is picked up in the pair of floral-on-blue pillows in the middle of the pile. Because they often incorporate botanical imagery, toiles pair well with floral patterns.

How to Create a Striking Mix

❶ Prominently position the main inspiration for a room's overall décor; in this case, it is the matching twin bedspreads.

❷ Use blocks of solid color in the area immediately surrounding an especially graphic print so the print itself can take full attention. Fuchsia bed skirts, pale green blankets, and pink shams with orange trim are seen here. Polka-dot pillowcases add an extra layer of pattern.

❸ Have at least one other piece of furniture in the room that repeats the full color scheme of the dominant pattern. The armchair's lively stripe brings in all the hues found on the beds.

❹ Try a completely different pattern at the windows, but use enough of it so that the end result is equal in visual strength to the room's focus pattern.

In this sunny sanctuary, the bed is abloom with tiny flowers. A checked blanket at the foot of the bed and striped and solid pillows interspersed with floral prints enliven the mix of patterns. Beyond bedding and seat cushions, floral patterns embellish numerous accessories around the room. Flowers adorn a collection of embroidered hankies and tea towels on a quilt rack, for example, as well as two fabric remnants that were framed and hung above the vanity. A floral-print curtain was attached to the wall in the far corner to mask a doorway leading to another room.

Decorated in a classic blue-and-white color scheme, this elegant bedroom features a number of floral patterns. A lively rose print covers the walls above the wainscoting, while a larger design was chosen for the curtains and window-seat cushion. Floral motifs also adorn the lamp base and bed frame; keep an eye out for furnishings like these when browsing antiques shops and flea markets.

Dramatic spaces can handle bold colors and strong graphics. The high ceilings in this hallway, for instance, stylishly accommodate the large-scale floral wallpaper; its deep plum blooms are outlined by apple-green woodwork. Floors, furnishings, and artwork are kept simple to balance the vibrancy of the walls.

◄◄ **TIP** *Installing wainscoting along the lower half of the walls and wallpaper on the upper half allows the wainscoting to keep the wallpaper pattern in check and give the eyes a place to rest. In addition, it will also cut your wallpaper costs nearly in half.*

It's possible to add just a hint of floral to a room and protect your furniture at the same time. On this settee, padded covers made from green-and-cream rose fabric rest on top and bottom of the seat cushion; ties of a generous length add visual interest.

◄┼ **TIP** *Slipcovers can instantly transform the ambience of a room. They can be tightly fitted and tailored, or casual and loose fitting. Use them to change the look of your pieces seasonally, to protect fine furniture, or just for fun.*

Decorating with Quilts

Not only are quilts icons of country style, they also possess a graphic presence few household accessories can match. So strong are those graphics, in fact, that quilts often hang on the walls of museums. In your home, these textile treasures can have an impact just as striking. And with the wide variety of patterns to be found, it's safe to say that there is a quilt that will complement any décor.

Laying a quilt on top of a bed is just the tip of the iceberg when it comes to displaying quilts in the home. Hanging them on the wall is another popular example; to distribute weight evenly, attach a fabric

sleeve to the upper back of the quilt. Other ideas include draping a quilt over the back of a chair or sofa, draping a selection on a quilt rack, and stacking them in a country cupboard. Time-worn quilts can even be salvaged and reinvented as upholstery fabric for a chair, ottoman, or footstool or as a pillow sham on top of a bed. Keep an eye out for unfinished quilt blocks at flea markets and rummage sales; frame a group for an eye-catching wall arrangement.

A single floral pattern can set the tone for an entire room, if that pattern is as bold as the 1950s needle-point rug in this country interior. The energy of this nasturtium design is reflected in the playful mix of furnishings up above, from the tall grandfather clock to the gilded convex mirror to the half-table with graphic diamond border. The flowing peach-colored drapes find a counterpoint in the rug's deep orange hues.

Colorful pottery with hand-painted flowers fills a roomy cupboard. Concentrated displays of floral collections look wonderful in rooms decorated with floral patterns. A single lidded jar from this cupboard or a smaller grouping would be equally attractive on a tabletop or mantel.

CHAPTER FOUR

Pictorials

If a picture is worth a thousand words, then the interiors on the following pages speak volumes. Each showcases pictorials—patterns that depict realistic or stylized images of people, animals, insects, seashells, fruit, urns, and so on. Few pattern categories are as versatile as pictorials. They encompass widely different looks, like airy toiles and hand-blocked historic wallpapers. They can play a supporting role in a room (a row of painted stars near the ceiling, perhaps) or be the focal point (a bold print covering the walls or upholstering the sofa). Pictorial patterns can even tell the world who you are and what you love by featuring images of hobbies (fly-fishing, horseback riding, travel) and pets (pugs, parrots, Persians).

Wallpaper offers an almost limitless amount of choices when it comes to pictorial patterns for the home. Some are realistic depictions of people, animals, garden tools; others—like this repeating foliage motif—are more abstract. When using a busy allover pattern such as this, opt for a pared-down style for furniture and accessories. Here, an off-white upholstered side chair stands beside a simple dresser painted spring green. The gentle curves of blown-glass bell jars reflect the flowing lines of the wallpaper.

Toile may be the best known—and most frequently used—of all pictorial patterns. Immediately recognizable by its finely engraved pastoral scenes set on a white or off-white ground, toile was first made in France in the late 1700s. As its popularity grew, production of toile spread throughout Europe and eventually to the United States. Red and white, blue and white, and black and white are among the most common colors, but green, sepia, mulberry, and other hues can also be found. In the home, toile can be used in any room, from private sanctuaries like bedrooms, dressing rooms, and baths to public spaces—living room, dining room, kitchen, foyer. Owing to their nostalgic feel, toile seems most comfortable in traditional decorating schemes and is rarely found in stark, contemporary settings.

When upholstering with pictorial fabrics, it is important to identify the pattern repeat, or the complete design unit that is repeated down the length of the fabric. Knowing where a repeat begins and ends will help you determine how much yardage you'll need for upholstery. Analyze placement possibilities before starting any upholstery project; center the dominant imagery (the figures or animals in a toile pattern, for instance) on a sofa or chair back, an accent pillow, or a head- or footboard. Busy patterns need little in the way of embellishment; solid throw pillows or curtain tiebacks that pick up a secondary color in the fabric add just the right note.

Some pictorial fabrics, like damask, are reversible, with the motifs in the front appearing in the opposite color scheme on the back. Patterns like these can be used to create unique decorating schemes. You might use the front of the fabric to upholster a sofa, while using the back for the pillows. Likewise you might choose the front for drapes, the back for tiebacks, or the front for a duvet, the back for a bed skirt.

Pictorials can be paired with any of the other patterns seen in this book. Toile especially, being such a classic country look, is often placed alongside checks or stripes. Toiles and florals can be mixed as well; a simple, open floral pattern works best since toiles are themselves busy patterns. When combining multiple pictorial patterns, stick with a single theme—variations on dogs, fruit, or Wild West imagery, for example—for the most cohesive look.

Many wallpaper patterns are offered with matching fabrics, expanding the decorating possibilities for people who love a coordinated look. Blue-and-white wallpaper depicting two Jane Austen-era friends with their babies gives a sense of continuity to the low, uneven ceiling. Identical fabric was used for the bedspread and bed skirt, cushions on the wicker rocker and couch, and curtains. An antique quilt in a deep indigo adds an extra layer of pattern to the foot of the bed. Blue carpeting lays a solid foundation underfoot.

A portion of a historic home's original interior paneling was the inspiration behind this living room's decorative painted pattern that incorporates leaves, hearts, and stylized flowers. The walls' faded-rose base color and the applied signs of wear and tear re-create an authentic atmosphere. To see other decorative paint motifs that might spark ideas for your own home, peruse books on Early American interiors or visit historic residences in your area.

Fanciful birds and urns filled with grapes adorn the walls in this bedroom decorated in typical Early American style. A commanding leaf border at the upper edge of the walls is echoed by a smaller design above the wainscoting. Traditional American art and crafts such as primitive portraiture, needlepoint samplers, and brightly-hued Blenko glass are ideal accompaniments to historic painted wall patterns like these.

When wallpapers display an especially strong graphic quality, there's no need to fill walls floor to ceiling to make an impact. In this country kitchen, a striking rooster motif wallpaper distinguished by broad bands of black covers the area above white beaded board reaching high on the wall. The predominance of white in the room balances the dark hue of the paper, while black details like the wire chairs, granite countertops, and wooden wine rack beside the refrigerator spread the color around the room.

Fabrics with pictorial patterns are good choices for slipcovers because you can center your favorite images on the backs and seat cushions of chairs and sofas, as the chairs surrounding this sunroom's glass-top table illustrate. Elegant covers like these can be used to dress up a table for guests, then removed for everyday use.

OPPOSITE: Toile's pastoral imagery makes it a natural choice for country interiors. An indigo toile fabric was applied to the walls of this dining area. Toile patterns often feature scenes of farming and harvesting, making them especially well suited to dining rooms and kitchens. Covers for the tops of the chairs were fashioned from striped fabric with a bolder blue; a long bag for baguettes hangs against the wall. On the floor, a tile pattern incorporates a floral image.

ABOVE: Because baths are generally small they are good places to experiment with pattern. You might feel more willing to try wallpaper with a larger motif or more vibrant colors than those you'd choose for the living room. If the result is not to your liking, there is less time and expense involved to change it. Cherubs, chariots, and other classical imagery distinguish this lovely gray design. Accessories like ornate gilded mirrors (formerly picture frames from Sweden, circa 1900) and crystal-embellished wall sconces reinforce the room's theme.

Papering the back of a cupboard or bookcase with a wallpaper pattern used elsewhere in the room is easy and attractive. This is also a wonderful way to make use of small amounts of vintage wallpaper that can sometimes be found at antiques shops or flea markets. If you love the pattern but there is not enough to paper an entire room, buy it anyway to use in this manner or for any number of similar projects: to line

drawers, paper a small closet, cover a hatbox. Papers that display faded colors or slight wear and tear complement antique furniture with timeworn surfaces.

◄◄ **TIP** *For an unexpected splash of pattern, line the inside of a bookcase, cupboard, or even a closet with leftover wallpaper or upholstery fabric.*

WHY IT WORKS

❶ Pictorial patterns can reveal a home-owner's passion; large-scale schooner wallpaper sets the theme for this sailing family's living room.

❷ A pair of armchairs upholstered in a matching print continues the room's nautical theme while picking up the blue of the wallpaper and the rose hue of the carpet.

❸ Roman shades in a simple plaid integrate a narrow grid of red, moving the color of the carpet around the room.

❹ Artwork and collections like the antique sailor portrait and the figurines act as finishing touches for the room.

Red and yellow is a beloved color combination, and one look at this elegant bedroom explains our enduring appreciation. Set against a backdrop of butter-yellow walls, a lively mix of red-and-white toile, florals, checks, and even a pink-and-white stripe grace the bed, chair, footstool, window bench, lampshade, and drapes. Notice how an image in the toile pattern is centered on the bed's throw pillows. To the left of the armchair, an antique bamboo armoire holds a collection of whole-cloth quilts. To spread the color evenly, the quilt with the most red is positioned at eye level with red details placed above and below.

An interior reminiscent of an English country manor is simple to re-create: Choose furnishings with subtly timeworn surfaces and dress them in a casual mix of fabrics that are old-fashioned in appearance. Toile is always welcome in such settings, especially designs that feature foxhunts and horseback riding like the example on the armchair. Though the fabrics used throughout the space are quite different from each other, a common color scheme of pale ocher and rose achieves a unified appearance. Antique-style portraiture and piles of books complete the look.

Bedding that incorporates old-fashioned silhouettes is a perfect focal point in a black-and-white bedroom. Fabric with portrait engravings was chosen for both the front and back of the armchairs; the striped fabric on the seats is mirrored in the drapes and roman shade over the desk. Subtle details underscore the color scheme; the bed frame is painted off-white while the chair frames are black. A black-and-white photograph of tulips and a graphic blanket at the foot of the bed add more layers of pattern to the décor.

Framed and hung above the bed, a pair of antique silk handkerchiefs depicts birds and a pastoral scene. Their delicate black-and-white imagery inspired the room's overall color scheme. On the bed, two narrow black stripes trim the pillowcases, a detail that complements the repeating floral pattern of the bedspread and shams.

◄◄ **TIP** *Frame printed handkerchiefs, remnants of beautiful fabric, or leftover wallpaper swatches and hang them on the wall like artwork.*

ABOVE: Toile looks at home in both formal interiors or casual country rooms. When upholstering with toile, center favorite images on chair backs, cushions, and throw pillows. If working with a set of chairs or a pile of pillows, position a different image from the fabric on each chair or on each pillow.

OPPOSITE: When including a graphic fabric in a room whose overall décor is dominated by soft colors, concentrate the fabric's use to a small area. In this living room, a bold blue-and-white fabric covers two footstools that have been pushed together to act as a coffee table. The love seat's pale blue color is echoed in the lampshade on the table beside the doorway; the pattern on the bolster pillow offers a middle ground between the visual strength of the footstools and the serenity of the love seat. Nail-head trim on the footstools adds texture to the pair.

PAINTED MURALS AND FLOORS

Introducing pattern into a house through painted walls and floors is a centuries-old tradition in the United States. In their earliest incarnations, decorative paint techniques gave homeowners of modest means a way to mimic the fine tapestries and marble flooring in wealthier homes. Simple checkerboard floor patterns were likely executed by the homeowners themselves, while highly detailed murals were generally the work of itinerant artists. The best known of these traveling painters is Rufus Porter (1792–1884), who painted landscape murals in private homes throughout New England.

Today, homeowners have enthusiastically revived the decorative painting tradition. Books on Early American interiors offer inspiration for patterns you might like to try in your own home. Like our ancestors, many people would feel comfortable attempting a checkerboard floor pattern by themselves (albeit with the assistance of a book on the subject, available at a library or art store) but would rely on a professional to create intricate murals. To find professional painters specializing in faux finishes, inquire at a local art store or historical society; ask to see a portfolio of past projects and to speak with former clients before any work begins.

Another popular decorative paint technique is that of stencil patterns, commonly applied to the upper portions or midpoints of walls. Kits can usually be found in art or paint stores, or even in bookstores.

The pleasing contrast between black and pale pink distinguishes this pretty bedroom. Because the fabric depicting old-fashioned silhouettes is graphically strong, its use for pillow shams alone is enough to make an impact on the whole room. A black-and-tan striped bolster echoes the lines of the striped ribbons on the silhouette fabric. A floral bedspread covers the bottom half of the bed, its hue picking up the pink in the silhouette fabric and in the antique embroidered child's book bag framed for safekeeping that hangs above the nightstand. A single silhouette on the wall ties the whole look together. Framed in a similar manner, any of the images from the silhouette fabric could also be displayed on the wall.

OPPOSITE AND ABOVE: Toile seat covers dress white-washed chairs in this bibliophile's dining room. The interplay between the elegant fabric and the distressed finish of the chairs is pleasing to the eye. Arranged on open shelves, a large collection of books takes on a pattern and color scheme all its own. A single needlepoint pillow depicting the homeowners' beloved breed rests on a purple velvet side chair nearby, further personalizing the space.

When one pattern in a room is particularly strong, it can anchor a lively mix of other prints. Here, the anchor pattern is most certainly the toile wall covering in deep raspberry and tan. Beneath it, twin four-poster beds sport identical bedding combining checks, plaids, and florals. Blue-and-white and red-and-white transferware platters dot the walls. Because transferware is made with engraved images just as toile is, layering one over the other invites closer inspection. To balance the energy of the multiple patterns in the room, windows wear only a simple curtain and floors are left bare.

In addition to Early American-style murals, hand-painted details also embellish numerous forms of antique furniture and accessories. Displaying even one example can be attractive, but positioning a group of painted pieces in a room brings to light the range of color and design created over the years. In this hallway, a landscape mural acts as a backdrop to a blanket chest and document box. A third, smaller painted box sits atop a dresser. Ocher was a popular color for floors in nineteenth-century country homes.

Using Pattern on the Ceiling

Ceilings may very well be the most overlooked part of the house. Usually they are painted white and left alone, but once they are adorned with wallpaper, fabric, or paint, their decorative potential becomes immediately apparent. In Victorian times it was quite common for ceilings (and every other surface in the house) to be covered with ornate wallpaper, but this seems to be the exception and not the rule when it comes to interior design in America. That is precisely why it can be such a wonderful surprise for guests to see pattern where they least expect it.

Which type of pattern to use will depend on a room's overall décor. In general, spaces should be somewhat pared down so they won't compete with a patterned ceiling, unless your goal is to re-create a period Victorian interior. The choice of pattern, too, should be simple and not overly busy. The red-and-white toile in this kitchen is a good example: the all-white cabinetry focuses attention overhead, and solid red elements like the work island, screen door, and dining room walls anchor the look. In addition to wallpaper or fabric (hiring a professional paperhanger is advisable for such a project), painted patterns like clouds or stars in kids' rooms offer even more possibilities.

One way that a widely varied mix of patterns can work together as a whole is to have a theme. The Wild West is the common thread in this colorful bedroom. Pillows with cowboys and an Indian head dress the bed. Furniture, accessories, and a graphic wall sign all contribute to the look.

OPPOSITE: Sometimes the imagery in a pictorial pattern can inspire the accessories and collections displayed in a room. Here, curtain fabric featuring portrait reproductions pairs well with antique silhouettes. Engravings would also have been a good choice. Carry a swatch of any fabric that will be a focal point in a room, as this one is, to help choose paint colors and other patterns that will share the space.

ABOVE: A green-and-white foliage pattern covers a chair and footstool in this cozy reading corner. A row of pressed leaves in frames mirrors the fabric's imagery up above. Creating similar artwork is easy to do: Simply collect leaves, press them in a dictionary, center them on a solid-color piece of paper, and fit them into a frame. Consider the texture of objects as another layer of pattern, like the rectangular motif carpeting.

The key feature that gives this bath beneath the eaves an air of elegance is the shower curtain fabric. Birds, flowers, and foliage are surrounded by a frame of stripes. The fabric's indigo-on-cream color scheme is repeated in the striped rug.

How to Create a Striking Mix

❶ Pick a two-tone color scheme, in this case black and white, and choose furniture and accessories that coordinate.

❷ Put your most vibrant pattern front and center, like the toile that upholsters the armchair cushions and armrests. Centering the rooster on the chair back draws added attention.

❸ Choose patterns of a smaller scale for other furnishings, like the gingham print on the window seat cushion and bolster.

❹ Find artwork and collections that complement the overall scheme. Black-and-white photographs are propped on an upper shelf, while polka-dot ceramics parade down below.

OPPOSITE AND ABOVE: One homeowner's passion for nineteenth-century wallpaper lead him to recreate historic patterns using traditional hand-blocking techniques. In his living room, repeating bands of white flowers on a background of sunflower yellow command attention. To balance the strength of the pattern on the walls, woodwork throughout the room was painted deep shades of sienna and black—colors that also would have been used in the 1800s. Furniture and accessories are also of the period; a grouping of wallpaper-covered hatboxes on top of the corner cabinet display other historic prints, such as a charming squirrel design. Color-coordinated collections spread the room's dominant hue around the room: a yellow tea set and a plate of lemons rest on a table beside the doorway leading to the kitchen.

⤙ **TIP** *Americans of the late 1700s and early 1800s generally chose the boldest designs for hallways, medium-scale prints for living and dining rooms, and subtle patterns for bedrooms.*

Deep reds and regal patterns give this cozy bedroom a much bigger feel. A Victorian interior come to life, the focal point of the room is a late-1800s canopy bed hung with curtains in a swirling floral pattern. On top of the intricate coverlet that dresses the bed itself is a pile of patterned pillows, including a needlepoint Dalmatian on a background of black. A needlepoint spaniel watches over the room from his frame above the bed. The walls display numerous framed examples of nineteenth-century needlework, bestowing pattern on every corner of the room. Every surface, too, holds visually intriguing arrangements, from the ribbed ironstone pitcher to the lower left of the bed, to the plaid box and woven basket to the right.

Often, mixing patterns successfully comes down to finding a common thread between varying prints; other times, it's fun to break the rules and simply combine as many patterns as possible. Though many of the fabrics inhabiting this vibrant bedroom share a cherry-red hue, the mix is delightfully irreverent, pairing florals, stripes, patchwork, and toile. A strong, solid color for the walls anchors the energy of the room.

A single armchair covered in caramel-on-white toile is one of the few patterned pieces in this rustic hide-away. An extra throw pillow covered in the same print rests on the yellow sofa, creating cohesion between the mismatched pieces. Consider the patterns found on everyday china and glassware. The cheerful floral glasses on the coffee table brighten the room; a large group of them would be eye-catching in a glass-front cabinet or on an open shelf.

A limited palette of plum, white, and red creates unity among a medley of patterns, including a classic toile at the window and a curvaceous botanical print on the oversized throw pillow. Here, the striped sofa cushion acts as a perfect counterpoint to the toile curtain up above; the band of red at the back of the sofa is underscored by the cushion's welting.

◄◄ **TIP** *When combining multiple patterns, stand back and consider the overall composition as a painter would view a canvas: be sure color and pattern flow evenly from top to bottom and left to right.*

ABOVE LEFT: Timeless paisley dresses an antique bed; its hues are picked up in the bed frame and the painted dresser right beside it. Though the origins of paisley lie in India, where the curved teardrop shapes were commonly woven into cashmere shawls, the name actually comes from the Scottish town of Paisley, where weavers reinterpreted the style and created highly sought-after designs of their own. Keep an eye out for vintage paisleys when browsing flea markets and antiques shops. Trays and platters bearing images of fruit, figures, and animals, like the exotic bird in this dresser-top display, are other treasures to search for.

ABOVE RIGHT: A toile sink skirt not only adds a touch of pattern to this country bath, it also provides hidden storage for soaps, towels, and toiletries. Just as this black-and-white fabric complements the room's neutral color scheme, other patterns might be chosen to coordinate with more vibrant interiors.

OPPOSITE: The beauty of pattern is that it can be used as abundantly or as sparingly as you like. In this serene bedroom, accent pillows add just a hint of pattern to the neutral space. The fruit-and-flower print evokes the grandeur of the natural world just outside the windows.

ABOVE: A tall ship, a windmill, fair maidens, and cityscapes are just a few of the pictorial images found in this collection of Staffordshire pottery. Its engraved appearance pairs well with toile and would be an attractive addition to any country interior. Examine the objects in your collection—painting a contrasting color inside the cupboard, cabinet, or bookcase where they will be displayed will make them stand out more.

OPPOSITE: Animal prints are among the most popular pictorial patterns. Rooster motifs are especially fitting in country kitchens—where families greet the day. These needlepoint rooster pillows adorn a red bench with a black-and-white checked cushion. The room's overall color scheme of black, white, and red is repeated in the checked rug and the smaller accent pillows on the bench.

Photography Credits

Page 2: Keith Scott Morton; Page 5 (left to right): Andrew McCaul; Keith Scott Morton; Michael Luppino; Robin Stubbert; Page 6: Lucas Allen; Page 8: Gridley & Graves; Page 10: Keith Scott Morton; Page 12 (left): Catherine Gratwicke; Page 12 (right): Gridley & Graves; Page 13: Keith Scott Morton; Page 14: Don Freeman; Page 15 (left): Lucas Allen; Page 15 (right): Keith Scott Morton; Page 16: Keith Scott Morton; Page 19: Gridley & Graves; Page 20 (left): Steven Randazzo; Page 20 (right): Andrew McCaul; Page 21: Robin Stubbert; Page 22: Jeremy Samuelson; Page 23: Robert Kent; Page 24: Keith Scott Morton; Page 25 (left): Keith Scott Morton; Page 25 (right): Michael Luppino; Page 26 (left): Jonn Coolidge; Page 26 (right): Grey Crawford; Page 27: Gridley & Graves; Page 28: Michael Luppino; Page 29: Michael Luppino; Page 30: Michael Luppino; Page 31: Keith Scott Morton; Page 32: Steven Randazzo; Page 33: Michael Luppino; Page 34: Keith Scott Morton; Page 35: Keith Scott Morton; Page 36 (left and right): Robin Stubbert; Page 37: Keith Scott Morton; Page 38: Keith Scott Morton; Page 39 (left and right): Robert Kent; Page 40: Michael Luppino; Page 41: Gridley & Graves; Page 42: Keith Scott Morton; Page 43: Keith Scott Morton; Page 44: Keith Scott Morton; Page 45: Frances Janisch; Page 46: Keith Scott Morton; Page 47: Natasha Milne; Page 48: Keith Scott Morton; Page 50: Natasha Milne; Page 51: Grey Crawford; Page 52 (top): Keith Scott Morton; Page 52 (bottom): Keller & Keller; Page 54: Keith Scott Morton; Page 55: Steven Randazzo; Page 56: Keith Scott Morton; Page 57: Jonn Coolidge; Page 58: Michael Luppino; Page 59: Keith Scott Morton; Page 60: Keith Scott Morton; Page 61: Jeremy Samuelson; Page 62 (left): Keith Scott Morton; Page 62 (right): Steven Randazzo; Page 63: Keith Scott Morton; Page 64: Robert Kent; Page 65: Keith Scott Morton; Page 66: Gridley & Graves; Page 67: Paul Wicheloe; Page 68: Gridley & Graves; Page 69: Andrew McCaul; Page 70: Peter Margonelli; Page 71: Jonn Coolidge; Page 72: Keith Scott Morton; Page 73: John Gruen; Page 74: Robin Stubbert; Page 75: Grey Crawford; Page 76 (left): Michael Luppino; Page 76 (right): Keith Scott Morton; Page 77: William P. Steele; Page 78: David Prince; Page 79: John Gruen; Page 80: Michael Luppino; Page 83: Steven Randazzo; Page 84: Don Freeman; Page 85: Jonn Coolidge; Page 86: Eric Roth; Page 87: Keith Scott Morton; Page 88: Michael Luppino; Page 89: Michael Luppino; Page 90: Michael Luppino; Page 91: Keith Scott Morton; Page 92: Keller & Keller; Page 93 (left): Robin Stubbert; Page 93 (right): Steven Randazzo; Page 94 (left): Michael Luppino; Page 94 (right): Natasha Milne; Page 95: Steven Randazzo; Page 96: Jonn Coolidge; Page 97 (left): Robin Stubbert; Page 97 (right): Andrew McCaul; Page 98: Keith Scott Morton; Page 99: Michael Luppino; Page 100: Michael Luppino; Page 101: Michael Luppino; Page 102: Michael Luppino; Page 103: Charles Maraia; Page 104 (left): Jeremy Samuelson; Page 104 (right): Keith Scott Morton; Page 105: Gridley & Graves; Page 106: Michael Luppino; Page 107: Michael Luppino; Page 108: Michael Luppino; Page 109: Michael Luppino; Page 110: Keith Scott Morton; Page 111: Charles Maraia; Page 112: Gridley & Graves; Page 113: Keith Scott Morton; Page 114: Michael Luppino; Page 115: Steven Randazzo; Page 116: Keith Scott Morton; Page 117: Steven Randazzo; Page 118: Steven Randazzo; Page 121: Keith Scott Morton; Page 122 (left and right): Keith Scott Morton; Page 123 (left and right): Keith Scott Morton; Page 124: Jonn Coolidge; Page 125: Robin Stubbert; Page 126: Robin Stubbert; Page 127: Gridley & Graves; Page 128: Keith Scott Morton; Page 129: Keith Scott Morton; Page 130 (left and right): Jonn Coolidge; Page 131: Robert Kent; Page 132 (left and right): David Prince; Page 133: Andrew McCaul; Page 134: Robert Kent; Page 135: Keith Scott Morton; Page 136: Keith Scott Morton; Page 137: Steven Randazzo; Page 138: Keith Scott Morton; Page 139: Keith Scott Morton; Page 140: Keith Scott Morton; Page 141: Gridley & Graves; Page 142: Keith Scott Morton; Page 143: Keith Scott Morton; Page 144: Keith Scott Morton; Page 145: Keith Scott Morton; Page 146: Keith Scott Morton; Page 147: Keith Scott Morton; Page 148: Keith Scott Morton; Page 149: Keith Scott Morton; Page 150: Keith Scott Morton; Page 151: Keith Scott Morton; Page 152: Keith Scott Morton; Page 153: Keith Scott Morton; Page 154 (left): John Gruen; Page 154 (right): Tria Giovan; Page 155: Don Freeman; Page 156: Keith Scott Morton; Page 157: Karyn Millet

Index